'2013'
Merry Christmas,
Ryan!

Love Always,
Grandma & Papa Bob

2013.
Merry Christmas.
Ryan!

Love Alicia
Grandma & Papa

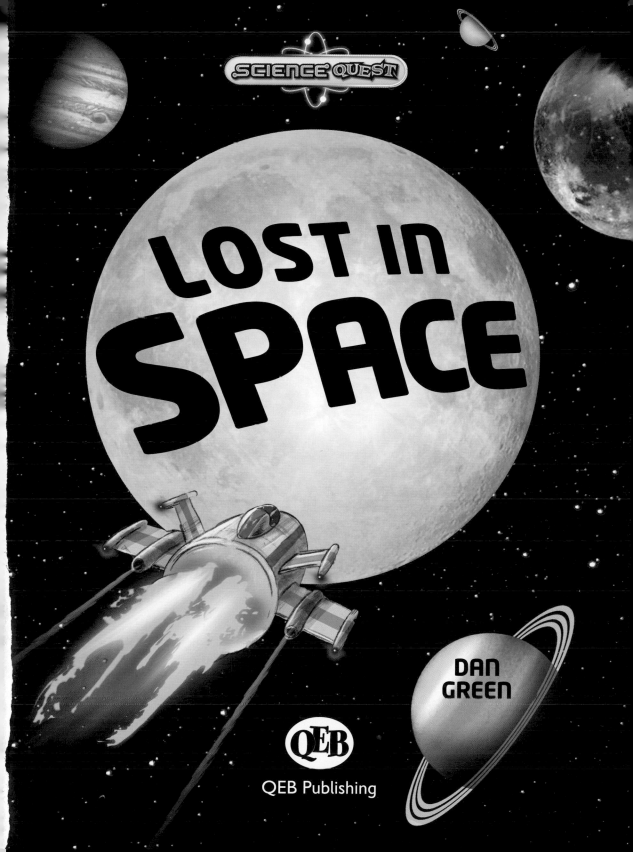

Cover Design: Mandy Norman
Illustrator: David Shephard
Editor: Amanda Askew
Designer: Punch Bowl Design
QEB Project Editor: Ruth Symons
Managing Editor: Victoria Garrard
Design Manager: Anna Lubecka

First published in the US in 2013 by
QEB Publishing, Inc.
3 Wrigley, Suite A
Irvine, CA 92618

www.qed-publishing.co.uk

A CIP record for this book is available from the Library of Congress.

ISBN 978 1 60992 507 9

Printed in China

Photo credits
NASA: NASA/JPL/University of Arizona, 1, 34, 40, 47; NASA, 13; NASA/
SDO, 46; NASA Johnson Space Center, 46; Steve Lee (Univ. of Colorado),
Jim Bell (Cornell University), Mike Wolff (Space Science Institute), and
NASA/ESA, 46; J.T. Trauger (JPL), J.T. Clarke (Univ. of Michigan), the WFPC-
2science team, and NASA/ESA, 47; NASA, ESA, and M. Showalter (SETI
Institute), 47; NASA/ESA and Erich Karkoschka, University of Arizona, 47
Shutterstock: bioraven, 5-43; ekler, 5-43; Monti26, 5-43; Palsu, 5-43
Science Photo Library: Ria Novotsi, 17

How to begin your adventure

Are you ready for an amazing adventure, full of twists and turns, that will test your brainpower to the limit? Then this is the book for you!

Lost in Space is no ordinary book— you don't read the pages in order, 1, 2, 3. . . . Instead you jump forward and backward through the book as the plot unfolds. Sometimes you may lose your way, but the story will soon guide you back to where you need to be.

The story starts on page 4. Straight away, there are puzzles to solve, choices to make, and clues to collect. The choices will look something like this:

IF YOU THINK THE CORRECT ANSWER IS A,
GO TO PAGE 10

IF YOU THINK THE CORRECT ANSWER IS B,
GO TO PAGE 18

Your task is to solve each problem. So, if you think the correct answer is A, turn to page 10 and look for the same symbol in blue. That's where you will find the next part of the story.

If you make the wrong choice, the text will explain where you went wrong and let you have another try.

The problems in this adventure are about planets and the Solar System. To solve them you must use your science skills. To help you, there's a glossary of useful words at the back of the book, starting on page 44.

ARE YOU READY?
Turn the page and let your adventure begin!

LOST IN SPACE

It's another ordinary day on board *Tin Can II*. Life as a patroller with PAWS (Police Agency for Wider Space) is nothing like the exciting adventure you thought it would be.

Suddenly the communicator crackles to life. . .

Ground Control to *Tin Can II*. We have an urgent mission for you. A spacecraft is in trouble near Pluto. We'd like you to investigate.

On my way, Ground Control.

Finally some action! With the flick of a switch, you fire the engines and roar off toward Pluto. . .

BLAST OFF TO PAGE 42 TO START YOUR ADVENTURE

It's icky, but true—until recently, the urine produced during 50 years of space missions was dumped in space, where it instantly froze into crystals.

TURN BACK TO PAGE 29 FOR ANOTHER SHOT

Mars is 142.5 million miles (230 million kilometers) away from Earth. Divide the distance to Mars by the speed of the car to find out how many hours your journey would take. 26 years isn't even close.

TURN BACK TO PAGE 36

Indeed, a meteorite is a rock that hits Earth. The biggest meteorite crater in the world is in South Africa. It measures 186 miles (300 kilometers) across.

You make it through the asteroid belt and across space to Mars.

You approach the ground too fast, landing with a bump and a scrape. *Tin Can II* has gone into **CRASH MODE** and has locked all the doors. You must answer a security question to open them.

CRASH MODE!

WHAT IS MARS' NICKNAME?

THE **RED** PLANET? GO TO PAGE 43

THE **RUSTY** PLANET? GO TO PAGE 20

You've got it! Solar flares are huge
explosions on the Sun's surface.
They can reach temperatures of up to
18 million degrees Fahrenheit!

There's a solar storm on the way and
it looks like it's going to be pretty mega.
Time to get inside.

But you put on your spacesuit in such a hurry
that all of your equipment's in the wrong place.
And you packed a few things by accident. . .

Quick, find these 10 items before the storm
hits: **glove**, **hand drill**, **wrench**, **hammer**, **pliers**,
clipboard, **pen**, **blueprints**, **magnet**, **oilcan**.

**ONCE YOU HAVE FOUND
ALL 10 ITEMS,**
GO TO PAGE 21

Being that close to the Sun, are you surprised that it's the hottest planet?! You watch as Mercury shoots past at 124,000 miles an hour (200,000 kilometers per hour). It is the speediest planet in the Solar System.

"Well done!" smiles the Professor. "Here's a mind-bender for you. Mercury turns so slowly that one day lasts longer than a year. True or false?"

THIS MUST BE TRUE.
TURN TO PAGE 23

NOT A CHANCE—YOU THINK THIS IS FALSE.
GO TO PAGE 19

Uh oh! Turtles, fruit flies, and mealworms were the first living things to orbit the Moon, aboard Russian spaceship Zond 5.

TURN BACK TO PAGE 32

Alpha Centauri is the *next*-closest star to the one you're looking for. You've got one more try before Rover's security system locks you out for good.

TURN BACK TO PAGE 37

The surface of Venus is hot enough to melt metal. Space probes that have landed on Venus have only survived for a matter of hours. With *Tin Can II* in the state it is, landing on this planet is best avoided.

TURN BACK TO PAGE 27

 Like astronauts aboard the International Space Station, you are in a standard 90-minute orbit, but thankfully you don't see 16 sunrises. After just a couple, you get clearance to finally go home. Dropping through Earth's atmosphere, you begin re-entry.

TURN TO PAGE 24

Mercury, Venus, Earth, and Mars are rocky, but not icy.

GO BACK TO PAGE 42 AND **TRY AGAIN**

Great stuff! Mars is named after the Roman God of War, and you've located the entrance to Crazy Pete's lair.

"Aaaaaaaaargh!" cries the Professor. A robot is guarding Pete's hideout!

Rover is not scared—for once. He recognizes that the robot is *Spirit*, NASA's old exploration rover from the twenty-first century. Pete must have programmed it to act as a guard dog! Mars Rover just flips *Spirit's* on–off switch and with a **ZZZZZP** the robot is quiet.

HEAD OVER TO PAGE 33

The four inner planets are small, rocky, and dense. Imagine what happens when you throw a rock into water—it sinks. So it can't be Earth.

All the planets—except the one that sits second from the Sun—spin counter-clockwise. Ceres isn't that close to the Sun! It's between Mars and Jupiter.

TURN TO PAGE 18 AND **GUESS AGAIN**

TURN BACK TO PAGE 16 AND **TRY AGAIN**

You're right. Astronauts wouldn't have used a map to get to the Moon!

The Professor tells you that the Moon isn't fixed.

What does he mean?

IS HE TALKING ABOUT **THE REBUILDING WORK AFTER THE 2010 STORM?** JUMP TO PAGE 26

DOES HE MEAN THAT **THE MOON IS SLOWLY CREEPING AWAY FROM EARTH?** OVER TO PAGE 13

Well done! The Great Red Spot is an enormous swirling storm, about 400 years old. It is so big that two or three Earths could fit inside it!

"You must get closer," demands the Professor.

Glancing down, you see the Great Red Spot on Jupiter's surface. You fly as close as you can, before quickly pulling up and away. The miners aren't so lucky. Their spacecraft spins out of control and is sucked into the eye of the storm.

WHAT A CLOSE SHAVE!
GO TO PAGE 41

Congratulations. Venus is the final correct answer. But you weren't fast enough, so one more...

What's my favorite food?

How are you supposed to know that? Think back. Have there been any clues?

SPACE CRACKERS?  GO TO PAGE 43

SATURN SQUIRMERS? GO TO PAGE 31

Yes, 262 long years!

Rover seems to be working but you'd better double check. You ask him another tricky question.

The astronomer Galileo was the first person to spot Saturn's rings—what did he think they were?

A HULA HOOP? GO TO PAGE 33

A PAIR OF STICKING-OUT EARS? GO TO PAGE 14

A SOMBRERO HAT? GO TO PAGE 20

 A king from Earth visiting Jupiter? Do you realize how far away it is?

TRY AGAIN ON PAGE 41

The boiling water and steam quickly melt the ice and you're free. You need information—and Flying Saucers is the place to get it. You point *Tin Can II* toward Neptune's largest moon.

Do you know its name?

IS IT TITUS?
GO TO PAGE 28

IS IT TRITON?
TURN TO PAGE 33

97? We're not talking about tiny space objects you know. Go lower!

GO BACK TO PAGE 20 AND HAVE ANOTHER POP

Wrong! Ham the chimp was a whiz at working levers to give him bananas in space.

FLIP BACK TO PAGE 32 AND **CHOOSE AGAIN**

The Moon isn't fixed in place. Amazingly, it's moving away from Earth at the same rate as your fingernails grow.

You are now in Low Earth Orbit, 1,240 miles (2,000 kilometers) above Earth. That's the same height as astronauts on the International Space Station.

If you stay in orbit for 24 hours, how many sunrises will you see?

24 SUNRISES—
ONE EVERY HOUR OF A 24-HOUR DAY.
GO TO PAGE 21

16 SUNRISES—
ONE EVERY 90 MINUTES.
GO TO PAGE 9

Ha ha! Galileo thought Saturn had ears! Crazy, but true.

Professor Brainstorm is staring out of *Tin Can II*'s front window. . .

GO TO
PAGE 26

Between the orbits of Mars and Jupiter is a belt of boulders.
Entering the asteroid belt requires a steady hand on the controls!
Even a slight scrape from one of these space rocks would be lethal.

Only the smartest travelers can navigate this belt safely. To steer
Tin Can II safely through the asteroid belt, answer this question:

WHAT DO YOU CALL A CHUNK OF ROCK THAT HITS EARTH?

**IF YOU THINK IT'S
A METEORITE,**
FOLLOW THE **LEFT ROUTE**

**IF YOU THINK IT'S
AN ASTEROID,**
FOLLOW THE **RIGHT ROUTE**

15

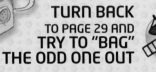

This bag of space tools was dropped during a repair mission in 2008—expensive junk!

TURN BACK TO PAGE 29 AND **TRY TO "BAG" THE ODD ONE OUT**

Dead end. Mars was named in ancient times before Melissa Mars was even born.

GO BACK TO PAGE 22 AND **TRY AGAIN**

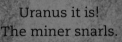

Uranus it is! The miner snarls.

You think you're sooo clever. Well, you'll never get this one.

Question three: Which planet rotates clockwise?

IF YOU THINK IT'S THE **DWARF PLANET CERES,** TURN TO PAGE 10

IF YOU GUESS **THAT IT'S VENUS,** ZOOM OVER TO PAGE 12

Bingo! You certainly wouldn't last long outside without a spacesuit.

The doors of the spacecraft have been blown off. You go in, and soon realize that this is an abandoned science survey ship.

Looking for clues, you make your way to the command unit and hit the power button. As the computer blinks to life, it asks for a password.

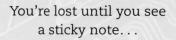

PASSWORD??

NAME THE FIRST PERSON ON THE MOON

You're lost until you see a sticky note...

CLUE:
Rearrange
Mr
Strong
Alien

IF YOU THINK THE NAME IS ARGON MINSTREL, FLIP TO PAGE 37

IF YOU COME UP WITH TRIANGLE NORMS, TURN TO PAGE 19

IF YOUR ANSWER IS NEIL ARMSTRONG, GO TO PAGE 39

How did you get this wrong? Laika the dog was the first animal to orbit Earth, in 1957.

GO BACK TO PAGE 32 AND **TRY AGAIN**

No, Jupiter and Saturn are the gas giants.

GO BACK TO PAGE 42 AND **TRY AGAIN**

67 is correct. That's a lot of moons to search! Saturn's largest moon, Titan, is bigger than the planet Mercury!

You rack your brains for ways to get free, when. . .

I'll set you free. But first you have to answer the three toughest questions in the Solar System.

Question one: What is the only planet that could float in a bath of water?

IS IT EARTH?
GO TO PAGE 10

OR **SATURN?**
TURN TO PAGE 43

OR **URANUS?**
JUMP TO PAGE 23

To conserve remaining fuel, you shut down the main engines. The computer gives you a quiz to pass the time.

WHICH PLANET WAS NAMED AFTER THE ROMAN GOD OF LOVE?

EARTH.
GO TO PAGE 31

VENUS.
GO TO PAGE 42

Sunrise to sunset on Mercury takes 176 Earth-days, while the planet moves around the Sun in just 88 Earth-days.

GO BACK TO PAGE 8 AND TRY, TRY, **TRY AGAIN**

PASSWORD??

<ERROR>

The password is incorrect, but the computer gives you another try.

GO BACK TO PAGE 17

YOUR SECURITY CLEARANCE HAS FAILED. YOU HAVE ONE ATTEMPT REMAINING.

CLUE

As well as keeping the Solar System spinning, this force also keeps your feet on the ground. It was discovered by Isaac Newton when an apple fell on his head.

TURN BACK TO PAGE 37 AND **TRY AGAIN**

You feel chains loop around your legs and hear a padlock close.

The spacecraft slows. You peek out of the porthole and see the rings of Saturn. The miners' hideout must be on one of Saturn's moons. If you ever get out of here, PAWS will need to search for the hideout—on every moon!

How many moons does Saturn have?

IF YOU GUESS **67**, FLIP TO PAGE 18

IF YOU THINK **97**, GO TO PAGE 13

The rings are like the rim of a sombrero hat. However, Galileo saw two smaller circles on either side of the planet. . .

GO BACK TO PAGE 12 AND INPUT THE NEW DATA INTO ROVER'S SYSTEM

Mars' nickname isn't the Rusty Planet. But you're nearly right—the reddish-brown color of the soil comes from rusty iron oxide.

PUT ON YOUR THINKING CAP AND **GO BACK** TO PAGE 5

More than 200 bags of trash have been dumped into space since manned missions began. The most famous piece of junk was astronaut Ed White's glove that he dropped while on a spacewalk.

GO BACK TO PAGE 29 AND **TRY AGAIN**

Spacecraft go around Earth every 90 minutes, which is 1.5 hours. Work out how many times the astronauts could orbit the planet in 24 hours.

$$24 \div 1.5 = ??$$

STRAP IN TIGHT AND **GO BACK** TO PAGE 13

Earth

90-minute orbit

International Space Station

50 years is incorrect. Check your math.

GO BACK TO PAGE 36 TO **TRY AGAIN**

The solar flare has safely passed, and so you continue toward Mercury.

The Professor is feeling a little bored so he suggests you play a quiz to pass the time.

Quiz question 1: What is Mercury known as?

THE **HOTTEST AND FASTEST PLANET.** GO TO PAGE 8

THE **SLOWEST AND COLDEST PLANET.** GO TO PAGE 26

21

So... Crazy Pete's secret base is *somewhere* on Olympus Mons— a dormant volcano and the highest mountain in the Solar System, three times higher than Mount Everest!

You, Professor Brainstorm, and Rover walk for hours until you reach a crossroads. You are tired, thirsty, and covered in red dust. You notice a large gray sign with a message written on it...

GO TO PAGE 16

GO TO PAGE 9

IF YOU THINK **IT'S NAMED AFTER THE ROMAN GOD OF WAR,** FOLLOW THIS ROUTE

To get to Crazy Pete's lair, answer this question.

If you get it wrong, you don't deserve to come.

How did Mars get its name?

IF YOU THINK THAT **A 12-YEAR-OLD GIRL CALLED MELISSA MARS NAMED IT,** FOLLOW THIS ROUTE

The biggest gorge in the Solar System is on Mars, but it's called Valles Marineris.

BACK TO PAGE 43 **FOR ANOTHER TRY**

 Ice giant planets are a little denser than water, so Uranus wouldn't float.

GO BACK TO PAGE 18 AND **TRY AGAIN**

Correct, it's true!

The last stop before Earth is the Moon.

Quiz question 3: Which one of these objects is not found on the Moon?

GOLF BALLS? GO TO PAGE 38

A SET OF PHOTOS? GO TO PAGE 28

A MAP? GO TO PAGE 10

For your amazing efforts in saving Professor Brainstorm and capturing Crazy Pete, you are awarded a medal and a promotion. Congratulations. . . **Colonel**! Mars Rover gets an oiling and a shiny new bone, and the Professor decides to have a holiday—on Earth.

Think about how close Mercury is to the Sun. Would this make it cold?

GO BACK
TO PAGE 21

There are no buildings on the Moon.

TURN TO PAGE 10 AND **SELECT AGAIN**

Uh-oh, wrong answer! An asteroid is a chunk of rock that never leaves space.

TRY AGAIN ON PAGE 15

Correct! Plus, on Earth, the force of gravity stops you from floating into space.

Just a few light-seconds into your journey, Tin Can II coughs, splutters, and breaks down. You probably should have filled up with fuel on Triton. Earth is currently on the far side of the Sun. Drifting home at this speed is going to take a long time.

TURN TO PAGE 18

FUEL

26

Correct! There are no inflatable crocodiles!

You'll need to investigate the damage the junk has done. Should you. . .

GO OUT TO SEE WHAT'S UP? TURN TO PAGE 38

LAND ON VENUS AND SEE WHAT REPAIRS ARE NEEDED. **TURN** TO PAGE 9

'Fraid not. Mercury doesn't orbit on its side.

GO BACK TO PAGE 43

That's correct! The planets in the Solar System orbit the Sun.

The recording starts to play. You see men climb on board and grab the Professor.

"Let's get back to Tin Can II," you say to Rover. *"We need to save the Professor!"*

Suddenly, the spacecraft shudders as a huge comet thuds into its side. **CRASH!** It's time to get out of here. You climb on board *Tin Can II* and try to disengage it, but ice has stuck the ships together.

What do you do?

BOIL WATER TO MELT THE ICE. GO TO PAGE 13

LOOK FOR SOMETHING TO CHIP AWAY AT THE ICE. GO TO PAGE 28

That will take hours! **CRASH!** Another comet hits *Tin Can II* with a mighty **BANG!**

BETTER TURN BACK TO PAGE 27 AND TRY AGAIN!

Nearly right. Neptune's biggest moon sounds very similar to Saturn's moon Titan.

TURN BACK TO PAGE 13 AND "TRI" A LITTLE HARDER

No, Earth is the only planet in the Solar System with just one moon.

GO BACK TO PAGE 42 AND TRY AGAIN

In 1969, the first men on the Moon—the *Apollo 11* mission—left a small aluminum disc there. It held a set of photos containing goodwill messages from world leaders.

HAVE ANOTHER TRY ON PAGE 23

That's right. Even though it has no moons, Venus is a real beauty. It is called the morning and evening star—depending on which time of day it appears in Earth's skies—and is the brightest thing in the night sky after the Moon.

You are admiring this lovely planet, when. . . **THWACK!** That sounded like a bump from some space junk.

Which of these bits of junk has never been found in space?

A GLOVE.
TURN
TO PAGE 20

A $100,000 TOOL BAG.
JUMP OVER
TO PAGE 16

AN INFLATABLE CROCODILE.
BOUNCE OVER
TO PAGE 27

TINY CRYSTALS OF URINE.
FLIP OVER
TO PAGE 5

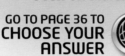 **Clue:** One year on Earth is 365 days. Divide the number of days in Mars' year by the number of days in Earth's year, and then multiply by the number of years Crazy Pete has been on Mars.

GO TO PAGE 36 TO CHOOSE YOUR ANSWER

 Not quite right. It may get a little windy, but that doesn't cause a solar storm.

GO BACK TO PAGE 38 AND CHOOSE THE CORRECT ANSWER

The cargo doors close behind you. Before you know it, you're leaving Triton. You hear voices getting closer. *Hide!* You clamber into a barrel just as a pair of miners enter the cargo bay.

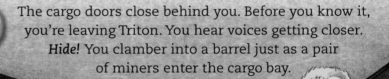

So 'ave we got the Proffff-essssor tied up?

Yup. We'll take him to Crazy Pete. He's at the Mons on Mars. He'll get the Prof to talk.

There's something in this barrel. It's slimy— and moving. . . Saturn squirmers! You can't believe people eat these. You let out a squeal. Rough hands reach into the barrel and pull you out.

TURN TO PAGE 20 TO DISCOVER YOUR FATE

Cracked it! There are two "ice giant" planets—Uranus and Neptune.

You're nearing Pluto, when you spot a drifting spacecraft. You can't see any signs of life, so you slowly pull alongside and prepare to board the craft.

You'll need your spacesuit, but why?

THERE'S NO OXYGEN IN THE VACUUM OF SPACE, SO WITHOUT IT YOU'D SUFFOCATE. GO TO PAGE 41

IN ZERO PRESSURE, YOUR BLOOD AND BODY FLUIDS START TO BOIL. FLIP TO PAGE 39

BOTH OF THE ABOVE. TURN TO PAGE 17

 Although you might love living on Earth, it was not named after the god of love. "Earth" means "the ground beneath our feet" in Latin.

TRY AGAIN ON PAGE 18

Saturn and Neptune are the right way around. Saturn is the big planet with large rings.

GO BACK TO PAGE 35 AND **TRY AGAIN**

You remember the barrels of Saturn squirmers—and push one over! The miner slips and drops the keys. They land at your feet! You unlock the padlock that's holding the chains around your legs and dash away.

RACE TO PAGE 32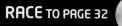

You must find the Professor before the miner sounds the alarm!

You round a corner and there, in front of you, is the Professor… locked in the dynamite storeroom! One false move and the whole place could explode!

To open the door, you must choose correctly on the keypad.

There's a clue written next to it.

CLUE:
Which of these animals has never been to space?

IF YOU THINK
A **CHIMP**,
TURN TO PAGE 13

IF YOU WANT
TO GO FOR A **DOG**,
GO TO PAGE 17

IF A **TURTLE**
SOUNDS RIGHT,
GO TO PAGE 8

IF A **SNAKE** IS
YOUR CHOICE,
GO TO PAGE 39

I should search this alone. Wait here.

You push hard on the door of Crazy Pete's lair and it flies open. You peer into the gloom.

YOU TAKE A DEEP BREATH, **STEP OVER THE THRESHOLD** AND GO TO PAGE 36

 A hula hooping planet? Come on—think properly!

GO BACK TO PAGE 12 AND **CHECK ROVER'S WIRING**

Here we are— Flying Saucers on Triton, the best ice-cream bar in the Solar System!

FLYING SAUCERS

This is where space-folk come to relax. If there's any information about Professor Brainstorm's disappearance, this is the place to get it.

YOU GET READY **TO BEAM UP** TURN TO PAGE 34

THE SUN

MERCURY

VENUS

EARTH

It's quiet tonight, but you take a seat and order an ice cream. Rover starts scanning the airwaves and before long, you catch a muttered conversation...

...KIDNAPPED
PROFESSOR BRAINSTORM...
DIAMONDS ON NEPTUNE...
HIDEOUT ON SATURN...

You are listening so hard, you don't see the barman return with the desserts.

34

The labels are in the right order, but which two models are in the wrong place?

SWAP JUPITER AND MERCURY.
GO TO PAGE 41

SWAP SATURN AND NEPTUNE.
GO TO PAGE 31

Jupiter is the largest planet—it is so big, 1,300 Earths could fit inside it!

You've lost the miners but you still need to recover the Professor's plans. You think they'll be with the miners' leader, Crazy Pete, on Mars.

<<BUZZZZZ>> Jupiter's strong magnetic field is making Mars Rover's computer systems act up. You'd better ask him some questions to see if there's any permanent damage.

If you were driving from Earth to Mars at 62 mph (100 km/h), how long would it take?

262 YEARS.
JUMP TO PAGE 12

NO LONGER THAN 26 YEARS.
GO TO PAGE 5

You walk down a dark tunnel. At the end is Crazy Pete, bent and crooked from years of working as an asteroid miner.

"The game's up, Crazy Pete," you say.

No! I owe money on Earth. If I go back without those Neptune diamonds, I'm dead. And I miss Earth. A year on Mars is the same as 687 Earth-days, and I've been here for 50 Mars years!

As you handcuff Crazy Pete, you do a quick calculation…

If Mars takes 687 Earth-days to travel around the Sun, how many Earth years has Crazy Pete been here?

GO TO PAGE 30 FOR A CLUE

NEARLY 95 YEARS. GO TO PAGE 37

ABOUT 50 YEARS. GO TO PAGE 21

"Is there someone there?"
you say in your bravest voice.

---WOOF!!! --- RZZUFFZ---

It's just Mars Rover, the Professor's robotic dog. You wonder if his camera recorded anything. You press play on Rover's control panel, but the Professor has set up a security system.

What is the name of the star around which all the planets in the Solar System orbit?

IS IT THE STAR ALPHA CENTAURI?
GO TO PAGE 8

COULD IT BE THE SUN?
TURN TO PAGE 27

<ERROR>
The password is incorrect, but the computer gives you another try.

GO BACK TO PAGE 17

That's 95 years away from all his family and friends on Earth! You drag Crazy Pete back to *Tin Can II* and prepare to head back to Earth. He'll be heading straight to a PAWS prison!

Back on *Tin Can II*, you contact Ground Control. You always forget your password, so you've written a clue on your dashboard.

Your password please, to verify your identity.

CLUE: What's the force that sets the planets spinning around the Sun?

IS IT GRAVITY?
GO TO PAGE 26

IS IT ELASTIC FORCE?
GO TO PAGE 19

You head outside to investigate. The Professor's voice crackles over the intercom system.

Captain, I'm seeing some unusual activity on the Sun. It could be a solar storm...

What is a solar storm?

EXPLOSIONS ON THE SUN'S SURFACE.
GO TO PAGE 6

HIGH WINDS AROUND THE SUN.
FLIP TO PAGE 30

NASA astronaut Alan Shepard played golf on the Moon in 1971. He left two balls up there.

HAVE ANOTHER SWING ON PAGE 23

No, Pluto is a dwarf planet, along with Ceres and Eris.

GO BACK
TO PAGE 42 AND **TRY AGAIN**

38

<CORRECT!>

NEIL ARMSTRONG WAS THE FIRST PERSON TO WALK ON THE MOON, IN 1969.

You start to look through the computer. It belongs to a "Professor Brainstorm."

You open a document marked

FINAL RESULTS: TOP SECRET

It says that conditions on Neptune may be enough to turn methane gas into diamonds. This research is worth a fortune.

You search the craft, but there's no sign of the Professor. Suddenly, something moves in the darkness.

TURN TO PAGE 37 TO SEE WHAT'S IN STORE. . .

It's true—fluids can spontaneously boil in zero pressure, so spacesuits provide artificial pressure to prevent a blood-boiling situation. But that's not all they do!

TURN BACK TO PAGE 31 AND TRY AGAIN

Correct! The door springs open. Just then, an alarm sounds.

"RUN!" you shout.

You and the Professor sprint down a tunnel, toward the exit.

You look up and there is. . .

JUMP TO PAGE 40 TO FIND OUT

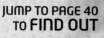

...*Tin Can II* with Mars Rover at the controls! Saved!

You jump on board and give the robotic pooch a tickle behind his ears.

You race toward Saturn. The miners are in hot pursuit and are closing in fast. A few more minutes and they'll be upon you. Scooting around Saturn's rings, you start programming *Tin Can II* to make a 354-million-mile hyperspace-jump to the next planet.

I've got it! Fly close to Jupiter's Great Red Spot— they won't dare follow you!

What is this planetary pimple the Professor speaks of?

IF YOU THINK IT'S A **400-YEAR-OLD STORM,** GO TO PAGE 11

OR **AN ENORMOUS VOLCANO,** TURN TO PAGE 42

Yes, a spacesuit provides an astronaut with essential oxygen. But it does so much more than that.

SCOOT BACK TO PAGE 31

The King is our savior!

He must mean Jupiter, but why does he call Jupiter the "King"?

IS IT BECAUSE
JUPITER WAS VISITED BY A KING?
TURN TO PAGE 12

IS IT BECAUSE JUPITER IS
THE **BIGGEST PLANET** IN THE **SOLAR SYSTEM**?
TURN TO PAGE 36

Brilliant work—Jupiter is the largest planet in the Solar System, so it's easy to spot when it's out of place!

While you've been busy, Rover has spotted the kidnappers—and they're leaving right now! You follow them to their ship and sneak aboard, while Rover stays on *Tin Can II*.

DIVE INTO THE CARGO HOLD
AND TURN TO PAGE 30

Venus and love go hand in hand!

You decide to attempt a gravity slingshot around Venus, which will take you close to the Sun.

You must watch out for moons, but how many moons does Venus have?

DO YOU THINK IT HAS ONE MOON, JUST LIKE EARTH?
IF SO, GO TO PAGE 28

YOU'RE SURE THAT VENUS HAS NO MOONS.
TURN TO PAGE 29

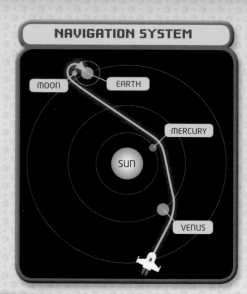

NAVIGATION SYSTEM

MOON
EARTH
MERCURY
SUN
VENUS

You peer at the Great Red Spot through *Tin Can II*'s periscope. You see fast-moving clouds spinning and swirling. . . just like a hurricane on Earth.

RETURN TO PAGE 40 AND TRY AGAIN

Thank goodness for something to do. It's probably just a spacecraft that's run out of fuel, but you're glad to have a mission.

To keep your brain from turning to jelly, you play a game.

SPACE QUIZ

Which are the icy planets?

URANUS AND NEPTUNE.
GO TO PAGE 31

JUPITER AND SATURN.
TURN TO PAGE 18

MERCURY, VENUS, EARTH, AND MARS. JUMP TO PAGE 9

PLUTO. GO TO PAGE 38

You're pretty smart. Saturn would float because it has a low density.

You can't get a bath of water that big, stupid! Ha ha haaaaaa!

Question two: Which planet orbits the Sun on its side?

IS IT URANUS?
GO TO PAGE 16

OR MERCURY?
TURN TO PAGE 27

Red it is! Now you're here, you must locate Crazy Pete and recover Professor Brainstorm's secret plans. Luckily you overheard the miners talking about "Mons," which you know means Olympus Mons.

But what is Olympus Mons?

IF YOU THINK IT'S A
REALLY BIG MOUNTAIN,
HEAD OVER TO PAGE 22

IF YOU THINK IT'S A
VERY DEEP GORGE,
ZIP TO PAGE 23

Space crackers? Good guess, but they're no one's favorite.

GO BACK TO PAGE 12
AND **GIVE IT ANOTHER TRY**

GLOSSARY

Asteroid

A rocky object that orbits, or circles, the Sun. Asteroids can be as tiny as pieces of dust or as large as a small planet. Most asteroids cluster together in the asteroid belt between Mars and Jupiter.

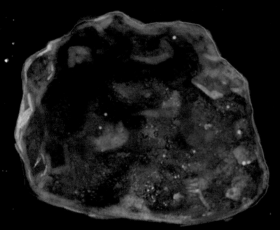

Rocky objects floating in space are called asteroids

Astronaut

A person who travels into space.

Astronomer

A person who studies the universe.

Atmosphere

The layer of gases surrounding a planet. Earth's atmosphere contains oxygen, which allows humans to breathe.

Comet

A small chunk of ice and dust that orbits the Sun. As it melts, gas and dust stream out into space to form its tail. It leaves a trail as it travels across the sky.

Crater

A bowl-shaped hollow on the surface of a planet or moon. Craters form when rocks from space crash into a planet.

Density

How much material is contained in a certain volume of an object. The denser an object is, the heavier it feels. Dense objects sink in water, and objects that are less dense than water float.

Dwarf planet

A ball of rock, such as Pluto, that orbits the Sun. Dwarf planets are too small to be classed as planets.

Gas giant

A planet made of gases with a small, rocky core. Gas giants are enormous—more than 10 times the size of Earth. The two gas giants in the Solar System are Jupiter and Saturn.

Gravity

A pulling force that acts between all objects in the universe.

Gravity slingshot

Using a planet's gravity to change the course or speed of a spacecraft's orbit.

Great Red Spot

A huge 400-year-old storm on Jupiter.

Ice giant

A large planet made up of ice. The two ice giants in the Solar System are Uranus and Neptune.

Inner planet

A planet made mostly of rock. The four inner planets of the Solar System are called the terrestrial planets—Mercury, Venus, Earth, and Mars.

Mercury is one of the inner planets

International Space Station (ISS)

A giant space station that was built in space. Here, astronauts can live and work for several months at a time. Its first component was launched in 1998. It was completed in 2011.

Magnetic field

Some planets have a magnetic field, which is like a bar magnet running through the middle of the planet from the north to the south pole. This field protects the planet's surface from harmful particles coming from the Sun.

Meteorite

A chunk of rock from space that lands on the surface of a planet or moon.

Methane

A colorless gas found on Earth. On the cold outer planets, methane is a liquid.

Moon

A large lump of rock that orbits a planet. Earth has one moon.

Orbit

When something loops around another object in space, it is said to be orbiting it. The Moon orbits Earth and Earth orbits the Sun.

Planet

A large, round object that orbits a star.

Pressure

The strength of the force with which something presses.

Solar

To do with the Sun.

Solar flare

Huge explosion on the Sun's surface.

The Sun

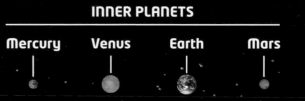

INNER PLANETS

Mercury   Venus   Earth   Mars

Solar System

The Sun and everything that orbits around it. The Solar System includes eight main planets, three dwarf planets, moons, asteroids, comets, meteors, and dust. They are all held in their orbits by the pull of the Sun's gravity.

Space

Everywhere beyond Earth's atmosphere.

Spacecraft

A vehicle, such as a rocket, that can travel into space.

Space junk

Any trash in orbit around Earth, including old rockets and satellites.

Spacesuit

A special suit that protects an astronaut in space. It keeps the body cool and supplies oxygen, so the astronaut can breathe.

Star

A large ball of hot gas that gives off light and heat.

Universe

All of space and everything in it.

Zero pressure

There is no matter in space, so there is no pressure. Liquids in your body, such as blood, boil almost instantly in zero pressure. This is why astronauts wear pressurized spacesuits.

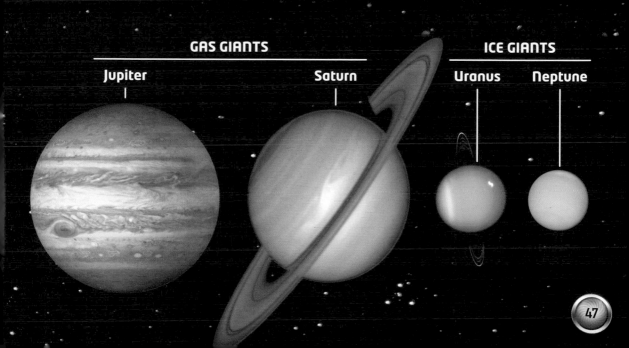

GAS GIANTS

Jupiter   Saturn

ICE GIANTS

Uranus   Neptune

Taking it further

The Science Quest books are designed to motivate children to develop their Science, Technology, Engineering, and Mathematics (STEM) skills. They will learn how to apply scientific know-how to everyday life through engaging adventure stories. For each story, readers must solve a series of scientific and technical puzzles to progress toward the exciting conclusion.

The books do not follow a page-by-page pattern. Instead, the reader jumps forward and backward through the book according to the answers given to the problems. If their answers are correct, the reader progresses to the next stage of the story; incorrect answers are fully explained before the reader is directed back to attempt the problem once again. Additional support is included in a full glossary of terms at the back of the book.

To support your child's scientific development you can:

- Read the book with your child.

- Continue reading with your child until he or she has understood how to follow the "Go to" instructions to the next puzzle or explanation, and is flipping through the book confidently.

- Encourage your child to read on alone. Prompt your child to tell you how the story develops and what problems he or she has solved. Take the time to ask, "What's happening now?"

- Discuss science in everyday contexts. Follow the changing phases of the Moon, star patterns, and the passage of planets through the night sky.

- Play STEM-based computer games with your child and choose apps that feature science topics. These hold children's interest with colorful graphics and lively animations as they discover the way the world works.

- Most of all, make science fun!